HOMEMADE

30 Recipes for Beginners

William David Welch

INTRODUCTION

Bread has been around for thousands of years. From its humble beginnings, satisfying hungry farm laborers and peasants, bread has nestled its way into the hearts of people everywhere.

You'll often find bread at the center of a meal. Arguably, the universality of bread makes it so appealing. No matter where you find yourself in the world, you'll be able to find a loaf of bread in one form or another.

Considering that at it's core bread is made from only four ingredients, it can be made in a hundred different combinations, all equally unique and delicious.

Over the last few years, breadmaking has become increasingly popular. It is something that people are falling in love with all over again. Its homeliness, heart, and warmth are things we all want to create in our lives.

This book includes 30 bread recipes that will serve as your introduction to the basics of crafting bread. From traditional loaves, to family favorites, to artisan delights, this book will make you fall in love with the art of baking bread.

Contents

CHAPTER ONE:
CLASSIC BREADS

COUNTRY BREAD

Le pain de campagne or French Sourdough

Also known as peasant bread, it comes in a variety of shapes and sizes and is usually dusted in flour or rye flour.

INGREDIENTS

Starter
1kg Bread Flour
600ml Warm Water
20g Fresh Yeast

Final Kneading
1.8kg Cake Flour
1.2L Water
50g Salt

METHOD

This makes a very wet dough, so it's a good idea to use your mixer.
Prepare the starter by mixing the flour, water, and yeast together.
Allow it to rest for five hours in a warm place.
Once it has rested, knead the starter into the cake flour, water, and salt.
Rest the dough for another half an hour.
Push the dough down and rest for another 20 minutes. Form into pre-shapes and rest for a further 25 minutes.
Re-shape the dough into its final shapes and rest for one hour.

BAKING

Steam cook your loaves first. This will help the bread to stay moist inside with a nice crusty outside.
Place a cast-iron pan onto the bottom shelf in the oven.
Heat the oven to 500°F for about an hour.
Place the bread in the oven.
Pour a cup of water into the pre-heated pan and close the oven door.

Allow the bread to steam bake for 15 minutes.

Remove the pan and allow the bread to dry bake for the remainder of the time.

Nutrition: Serving: 1 slice (43g) | Calories: 120 kcal

BAKER'S TIP

Make sure to properly score your bread before you bake it. Scoring helps give the bread room to expand in the oven.

PANE FRANCESE

Also called French Bread

Despite what the name might suggest, this bread actually originated in Northern Italy. Its name translates into "French bread." It is a style of French country bread.

INGREDIENTS

The ingredients are categorized into two sections: biga and the final dough.

Biga
280g Bread Flour
160g Warm Water
10g Fresh Yeast

Final Dough
400g Bread Flour
290g Water
10g Salt

METHOD

Start off by making the biga.
Add the bread flour, warm water, and yeast together.
Knead and then roll into a round ball.
Lightly oil the ball and leave it in a sunny (warm) spot.
Wait for it to double in size.
Cut the biga into small pieces and add it to the water for the final dough. This will help to fortify the biga and make the distribution more even.
Mix the final dough with the biga and knead by hand.
Oil a large container and place the dough inside to proof until it has doubled in size.
No stretching or folding of the dough is necessary for this recipe.
Cut the dough into neat squares (16-20).
Do a final proof (1 to 2 hours).
Score the dough with a single cut.
You may choose to seed or flour the bread if desired.

BAKING

Ideally you want to do a steam-cook first.
Place a cast-iron pan onto the bottom shelf in the oven.
Heat the oven to 500°F for about an hour.
Place the bread in the oven.
Pour a cup of water into the preheated pan and close the oven door.
Allow the bread to steam bake for 15 minutes.
Remove the pan and allow the bread to dry bake for the remainder of the time.

Nutrition: Serving: 1 slice (45g) | Calories: 100 kcal

BAKER'S TIP

How to tell if your bread is ready:
It should have a good rise, a lovely golden color, and a nice hollow sound when you tap the bottom.

RYE BREAD

Rye bread has been baked around the world for hundreds of years. Rye was a good ingredient to use because it grows well in cold conditions and poor soil. Nowadays, rye bread is still popular and is rich in fiber and flavor. It also has less gluten than white bread.

INGREDIENTS

Starter
1kg Bread Flour
600ml Warm Water
50g Fresh Yeast

Final Kneading
750g Rye Flour
500ml Water
25g Salt

METHOD

The rye dough has a propensity to break apart, so don't overdo the kneading.
Also, as rye has a lower gluten level than other flours, it will take longer to rise. Prepare the starter by mixing the flour, water, and yeast together.
Allow it to rest for two hours in a warm place.
Once it has rested, knead the starter into the rye flour, water, and the salt.
Rest the dough for half an hour.
Push the dough down and rest for another 20 minutes.
Shape the loaf and allow it one final proof. Half an hour should do.
Preheat the oven to 425°F.

BAKING

Score the bread before putting it in the oven.
Place the bread in the oven.
Bake for 30 minutes.

Turn the oven down 5 minutes before the bread is ready to come out.

Nutrition: Serving: 1 slice (32g) | Calories: 83 kcal

BAKER'S TIP

Throw a few ice cubes into the bottom of your oven to create a bit of steam.
It'll do wonders for your bread and help you to create a beautiful crust.

TRADITIONAL BRIOCHE

Brioche is a delicious bread known for its distinctive sheen and buttery flavor.

INGREDIENTS

830g All-Purpose Flour
10g Active Dry Yeast
80ml Warm Water
15g White Sugar
5g Salt
4 Eggs
250g Butter (Softened)
1 Egg Yolk
10ml Cold Water

METHOD

Add the yeast to the warm water. Mix and allow to stand for 10 minutes.
In a large bowl, add the remainder of the dry ingredients (flour, sugar, and salt).
Make a well in the center and add the eggs and the yeast/water mixture. Mix until the dough has come together, then turn onto a floured surface and knead for about 8-10 minutes.
Flatten the dough on the counter and cover it in 1/3 of the softened butter.
Knead the butter into the dough. Repeat this process until all the butter is kneaded into the dough (3 x in total). The total time spent kneading the butter into
the dough will be about 15-20 minutes.
Lightly grease a large bowl and place the dough in the bowl. Turn it gently around until it is lightly greased. Cover with a damp cloth and let it rise in a warm place until double in size. This should be about 1 hour.
After an hour, deflate the dough, cover it in cling wrap, and place it in the fridge overnight.
The next day, place the dough back on the floured surface. Split it into two pieces and shape into loaves.
Grease two loaf pans and then place the shaped loaves into the pans.

Cover with a cloth and allow it to rise for another 60 minutes.
Preheat oven to 400°F.

Beat the egg yolk with 1 teaspoon of water to make a glaze.
Brush the two loaves with the egg wash.

BAKING

Bake for 25 minutes and then check the loaves. After 30 minutes,
they should be a nice golden brown.
Don't remove from the loaf pans immediately, allow them to rest for
10 minutes before transferring them to a wire track.
Cool completely before serving.

Nutrition: Serving: 100g | Calories: 346 kcal

BAKER'S TIP

You can flavor your brioche with chocolate chips, dried fruit, orange
zest, and other spices.

WHOLE WHEAT BREAD

A classic brown bread with a farm-style, traditional feeling.
Whole wheat bread is often made with nuts and seeds.

INGREDIENTS

1.8kg Whole Wheat Flour
80g Honey
10g Vegetable
Oil 20g Bicarbonate of Soda
10g Salt
1L Natural Yogurt

METHOD

Mix the dry ingredients together in a bowl.
Add the wet ingredients.
Mix all of the ingredients together well.
Divide equally into two tins (this recipe should give you enough for
two loaves of whole wheat bread).
Preheat the oven to 370°F.

BAKING

Place the bread in the oven.
Bake for 60 minutes.
Turn off the oven and leave the bread inside for an additional 15
minutes.

Nutrition: Serving: 100g | Calories: 247 kcal

Spice up your whole wheat loaf by adding seeds such as sunflower seeds, pumpkin seeds, and sesame seeds. They are a healthy and delicious addition to a lot of breads and offer a bit of texture.

CLASSIC WHITE BREAD

A traditional family favorite. Perfect as a sandwich bread.

INGREDIENTS

800g Bread Flour
10g Salt
2 pkts Active Dry Yeast
30g White Sugar
500ml Warm Water
30g Butter (Softened)

METHOD

Add the yeast and sugar to the warm water. Stir until dissolved. Then add in the softened butter, the salt, and 2 cups of flour. Stir.
Add the rest of the flour in stages, 1/2 a cup at a time, and mix well after each addition. Once mixed, place on a lightly floured surface and knead for 8-10 minutes.
Grease a large bowl and place the dough in the bowl.
You can turn the dough in the bowl so that it is completely coated in oil. This will stop it sticking to the sides of the bowl as it rises.
Cover with a cloth and leave in a warm place to rise for an hour.
After an hour, place the dough back on the floured surface.
Split it into two pieces and shape into loaves.
Grease two loaf pans and then place the shaped loaves into the pans.
Cover with a cloth for another 35-40 minutes.
Preheat oven to 425°F.

BAKING

Turn the oven down and bake at 375° for about 25-30 minutes. After 30 minutes, the bread should be a nice golden brown.
If you tap the bottom it should sound hollow.
Cool completely before serving.

Nutrition: Serving: 1 slice | Calories: 92 kcal

BAKER'S TIP

Keep a close eye on the oven. All ovens are different and sometimes one side of the bread may brown quicker than the other. You can always cover the bread with a piece of foil if it is getting too brown.

NO-KNEAD BREAD

This recipe is for "the bread that breaks all the rules." It's a very forgiving recipe and great for "free-style" bakers.

INGREDIENTS

Dough
1 kg Bread Flour, Plus Extra to Dust
5g Salt
10g Instant Dried Yeast
950ml Lukewarm Water

Topping
Fresh Rosemary
Sea Salt

METHOD

Combine flour, salt, and yeast in a large bowl. Stir in water until well-combined.
Cover with plastic wrap, then refrigerate overnight.
Remove bowl from fridge 1 hour prior to baking, and allow to come to room temperature.
Preheat oven to 430°F.
Line two baking sheets with baking paper and generously dust the sheet with flour.
The dough can be quite wet. Make sure that your hands are wet, as well as the implements you are using to make it easier to handle.

BAKING

Place half of the dough onto one tray, sprinkle with rosemary and sea salt, and place in the oven for 1 hour or until golden and the inside sounds hollow when knocked on the base.

Make rolls and a smaller long loaf with remaining half of dough. Sprinkle with rosemary and sea salt. Bake in the oven for about 40 minutes or until golden outside and hollow-sounding inside.

Nutrition: Serving: 1 slice | Calories: 120 kcal

BAKER'S TIP

You can bake the bread in a loaf pan if you want a more structured loaf.
This bread makes the best toast!

CHEESE BREAD

A deliciously crusty cheese bread with a soft center.
Great for dinner parties or just for any old day.

INGREDIENTS

Basic Bread Dough
10g Sugar
5g Dry Active Yeast
75ml + 15ml Milk
100g Whole Wheat Flour

Cheese Bread Dough
3g Chili Powder
3g Ground Cumin
250g Shredded Cheese (a Strong Cheese like Mature
Cheddar or Lancashire)
750g Bread Flour
Beaten Egg - to Wash the Top of the Dough
125g Cup Grated Cheese for Topping

METHOD

First you must make your basic bread dough.
Dissolve the yeast into the sugar and milk, then slowly add the flour.
Roll into a ball and place in a greased bowl. Cover and leave in a
warm place to rise for one hour.
After an hour, you can make the cheese bread dough.
Add the spices to the shredded cheese, then add the basic
bread dough.
Combine until the cheese is spread evenly through the mixture. If the
dough is too tight, you may need to add a little water.
Separate the dough into six pieces and roll into balls.
Give them a few minutes to rest and then press down until they are
about twice the diameter they were before.
Line a baking tray with baking paper and place the flattened pieces of
dough onto the tray. Make sure you don't put them too close together.
Score by making a cross on the top of each disk. Press down hard
until the knife almost reaches the backing paper.
Brush with the egg wash.
Add the grated cheese evenly across them.

Be careful not to put it too close to the edges, as it will melt.
Preheat the oven to 375°F.

BAKING

Proof the three breads until they have risen nicely. Bake for 15-20
minutes. Be careful not to overcook the cheese.

Nutrition: Serving: 100g | Calories: 260 kcal

BAKER'S TIP

Cheese bread is a great addition to a variety of dishes including
pastas, soups, and chicken dishes.

SWEDISH NIGHTBREAD

INGREDIENTS

450g Wheat Flour
5g Salt
30g Sugar
10g Dry Yeast
250-300ml Warm Water
50ml Sunflower Seeds
50g Flax Seeds
Vegetable Oil

METHOD

Sift flour. Add all other ingredients.
Stir all the ingredients with a wooden spoon. The dough will be quite sticky, but don't worry.
Grease the loaf tin with vegetable oil. Remember to also grease the sides of the tin.
Line the loaf tin with baking paper.
Transfer the dough to the tin with a spoon, cover with a greased piece of cling film.
Place in the refrigerator for the night.

BAKING

In the morning, remove the loaf tin from the fridge.
Do not preheat the oven, but place the bread into a cold oven.
Set it to 430°F degrees and bake for 35-40 minutes.
The bread should be a nice brown color and when you tap the bottom there should be a dull hollow sound.

Nutrition: Serving: 100g | Calories: 239 kcal

BAKER'S TIP

Always knead bread with wet hands.

CHAPTER TWO:

ARTISAN BREADS

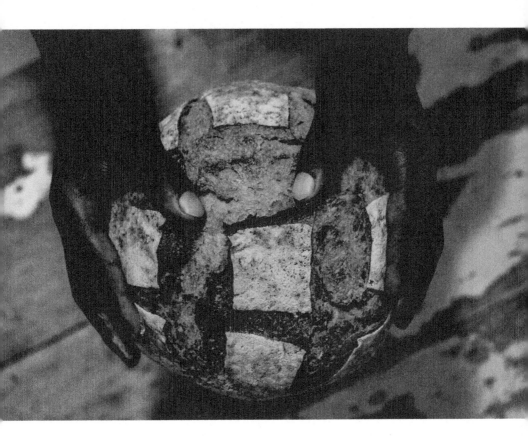

CIABATTA

A delicious rustic Italian bread, perfect for open-faced
sandwiches and soups.

INGREDIENTS

Sponge
165g Bread Flour
165g Warm Water
5g Fresh Yeast

Final Dough
300g Bread Flour
200g Water
10g Salt
10g Fresh Yeast

METHOD

Mix the ingredients to form the sponge and place it in the
refrigerator overnight.
Combine the ingredients for the final dough and then mix the sponge
in. Using a tablespoon of oil, knead the dough until it is smooth
and elastic.
You want the sponge to mix completely with the final dough.
Put it in a bowl to proof for one and a half to two hours.
Fold and stretch the dough. Divide into smaller shapes.
Place in the refrigerator to proof for another 20 minutes.
Dust with flour.
Preheat the oven to 425°F.

BAKING

Score the bread before putting it in the oven.
Bake for 20 minutes.

Nutrition: Serving: 100g | Calories: 240 kcal
.

BAKER'S TIP

Remember to plan ahead and make the sponge the day before.

HOMEMADE DUTCH OVEN BREAD

For those wanting to create the ultimate artisanal loaf of bread, this is the recipe for you.

INGREDIENTS

500ml Warm Water
1pkt Dry Yeast
1kg All-Purpose Flour
10ml Olive Oil
10g Salt

METHOD

Mix the water and the yeast together.
In a separate bowl, combine the flour and salt together. Make a well in the center and then slowly add the water/yeast mix.
Combine with your hands. If the dough is too sticky, wet your hands to make it easier. Once the dough is well-mixed, put it in a bowl, cover it, and let it rise for about 2 hours.
It should be twice the size it was originally.
Work the dough away from the sides of the bowl and fold the dough into the center.
Repeat until it is all folded in the middle of the bowl.
Cover again and let rise for another 2 hours.
After 2 hours, begin to shape the dough. Lightly dust a clean surface with flour and then shape it into a ball-like form.
Coat with olive oil and lightly dust with flour.
Cover the dough and let it rest for another hour.
Preheat the oven to 450°F.

BAKING

Place the Dutch oven (or heavy cooking pot) in the preheated oven for 50-60 minutes.

VERY carefully take the Dutch oven/pot out of the oven.
Put the bread into the pot.
Cover with the lid and put the pot back in the oven.

Bake the bread for 45 minutes. Remove the lid for the last 10 minutes. Remove bread and cool completely before serving.

Nutrition: Serving: Single Serving | Calories: 262 kcal

BAKER'S TIP

Spice up your whole wheat loaf by adding seeds such as sunflower seeds, pumpkin seeds, and sesame seeds.

SOURDOUGH BREAD

To make sourdough bread, you need to create a starter. This is a combination of water and flour that you leave over a period of time.

The starter makes "wild yeast," a naturally occurring process.

INGREDIENTS

500g Bread Flour
250ml Water
300g Sourdough Starter
10g Sugar
10g Salt
Vegetable Oil

METHOD

Combine the water, starter, and flour together.
Add the salt and the sugar to the mix.
Sprinkle some flour onto the counter and turn the dough out of the bowl.
Knead it with your hands until it is smooth and elastic.
Form the dough into a ball. Cover the ball in a thin layer of vegetable oil. Place it in a bowl, cover, and leave it to proof for 3 hours. After 3 hours, check on your dough and separate it into two halves. Place them into two lined bowls.
If the bowls are not lined, the dough will get stuck.
Proof for an additional 2 hours. Preheat the oven to 440°F.

BAKING

Steam cook your loaves first. This will help the bread to stay moist inside with a nice crusty outside.
Place a baking tray onto the bottom shelf of the oven and fill it with water or ice.
Score the bread before baking. Place the bread in the oven.
Bake for 40 minutes or until ready.

Nutrition: Serving: Single Serving (32g) | Calories: 92 kcal

BAKER'S TIP

You can keep your starter going by feeding it with flour and water.
This means you can bake bread whenever the urge strikes.

FOCACCIA

An Italian classic, focaccia is a delight to taste and in how simple it is to prepare. It makes a great snack or light lunch. Plus, there are so many variations on it that you'll never get bored.

INGREDIENTS

120ml Extra-Virgin Olive Oil
2 Garlic Cloves
20g Herbs (Thyme and Rosemary are Good)
235 ml Warm Water
12g Dry Yeast
5g Teaspoon of Honey
315g All-Purpose Flour
Ground Black Pepper
Sea Salt

METHOD

Cook the garlic, herbs, olive oil, and pepper in a pan until brown.
Combine the warm water, yeast, and honey. Let it rest for a few minutes.
Slowly combine the flour, salt, and 1/4 of the oil-garlic-herb mix with the yeast, water, and honey. Let it rest for a few minutes. Knead the dough until it is smooth.
Place the focaccia dough in a greased bowl, cover, and leave it in a warm area for 1 hour.
Place the two halves into two lined bowls. If the bowls are not lined, the dough will get stuck to the bowls.
Proof for an additional 2 hours.
Preheat the oven to 450°F.

BAKING

Add all but 2 tablespoons of the olive oil infusion to the bottom of a baking tray.
Make sure the baking tray is relatively deep.

Press the dough into the pan, making sure to leave little dimple impressions on the surface of the bread.
Oil the top of the focaccia with the remaining oil-garlic-herb mixture.
Bake for 18 to 20 minutes or until golden brown.

Nutrition: Serving: Single Serving | Calories: 262 kcal

BAKER'S TIP

Add olives, feta cheese, and cherry tomatoes for a Mediterranean twist.

HERB LOAF

This delicious no-yeast recipe is a delicious no-fuss bake.

INGREDIENTS

500g Bread Flour
20g Baking Powder
60g Whole Wheat Flour
50g Sunflower Seeds
20g Fresh, Chopped Assorted Herbs (i.e. Garlic, Chives, Sage,
Rosemary, Thyme, Oregano, Marjoram, Celery)
10g Chopped Parsley
15g Brown Sugar
15g Wheatgerm
500ml Buttermilk/Plain Yogurt (Room Temperature)
1 XL Egg (Room Temperature)
Paprika Powder

METHOD

Preheat the oven to 350°F. Grease and flour the bread tin. Add the
dry ingredients together.
Mix the beaten egg into the buttermilk/yogurt.
Combine the dry ingredients with the wet ingredients. Make sure they
are well-mixed.
The dough should be quite stiff.
Spoon the bread dough into the baking tin and sprinkle lightly with the
paprika powder.

BAKING

Bake for 1 hour in the middle of the oven.
After an hour, test with a toothpick/skewer to see if it's ready.

Cool completely before removing from the tin.

Nutrition: Serving: Single Serving (32g | Calories: 88 kcal

BAKER'S TIP

It's important to make sure you grease your bread tin well
beforehand.
Using butter or oil to grease it, and then adding a fine sprinkling of
flour helps to ensure an easy release after the bread has baked.

ROSEMARY BREADSTICKS

Breadsticks are versatile and can be easily stored and eaten with soups, pasta dishes, and dips.

INGREDIENTS

2 Cups Cake Flour
1 Tsp Dry Active Yeast
1 1/4 Cup Warm Water
3 Tbsp Olive Oil
1 Egg Beaten with
3 Tbsp Water
4 Tbsp Finely-Chopped Rosemary
Coarse Salt

METHOD

In a large bowl mix half of the flour, yeast, and warm water until smooth.
Add 3 tablespoons of the egg mixture and the rosemary.
Mix in the remaining flour (125g at a time) until you form a soft dough.
Knead for about 8 minutes on a lightly floured surface until it is smooth and elastic.
Grease a large bowl with olive oil, cover, and let the dough rise for 30 minutes.
Preheat oven to 390°F.
Once the dough has finished rising, you can separate it into two pieces. Roll each half out into a long "rope" about 40 cm in length.
Cut into 14 pieces.
Lightly grease a baking tray and lay the formed breadsticks on the tray.
Sprinkle with coarse salt.

BAKING

Bake for 15 minutes until the breadsticks are golden in color.
Transfer to a wire rack.
Cool completely before serving.

Nutrition: Serving: 1 breadstick | Calories: 107 kcal
Low Cholesterol and Low Fat

BAKER'S TIP

You can swap out the rosemary for another herb like cilantro. You can also use a combination of cake flour and wheat flour.

AUSTRALIAN VEGETABLE BREAD

A real crowd-pleaser. This loaf is as pretty as it is delicious.

INGREDIENTS

1kg Wheat Flour / Flour (Sifted) One Cup (250g) for 1 Type of
4 X Doughs
Salt (3/4 Tsp for 1 Type of Dough) - 3 Tbsp
Sugar (1 Tbsp per Type of Dough) - 4 Tbsp
Vegetable Oil (0.5 Tbsp per Type of Dough) - 2 Tbsp
40g Fresh Yeast (10g per Bread or Dry Only 1 Tsp or
3/4 per Bread)
110 ml Beetroot Juice
110 ml Tomato Juice
110 ml Spinach Juice
110 ml Water

METHOD

Make the spinach juice by adding a splash of water to the
juicer/blender along with the bunch of spinach. Blend until smooth.
Make the tomato juice. Add 100ml of water and 2 tbsp of
tomato paste.
Lastly, make the beetroot juice. Put 3 small beets into the juicer. Add
water if necessary.
Measure out 110ml of each juice. In in each glass, add 1 tbsp sugar
and 10g fresh or 3/4 tsp dry yeast. Mix together.
Make the plain bread dough. Add 1 cup of flour + water with sugar
and yeast + 3/4 tsp. salt + 0.5 tbsp vegetable oil.
Knead the plain dough.
Then add flour to the juices to make the 3 vegetable doughs.
Remember that you may need to add a bit more water or flour
depending on the gluten level in the flour, humidity in the kitchen, etc.
Cover with cling film and place in a warm spot to proof.
While the dough rises, prepare the baking pan. Grease with butter,
sprinkle with flour.
You can use a cast-iron skillet with high edges or a deep baking pan.
The dough should double in size in 40 minutes. Next, you need to
shape the bread.

Roll the bread into sausage-like shapes. Grease your hands with oil or add a sprinkling of flour to the table. Create a spiral formation with the dough.
Cover and leave in a warm place to rise.
Preheat the oven to 430°F.

BAKING

Bake for 45-55 minutes. Transfer to a wire rack.
Cool completely before serving.

Nutrition: Serving: 100g | Calories: 260 kcal

BAKER'S TIP

Did you know that 70°F is the ideal temperature to raise bread?
You should try to leave the bread in a temperature as close to 70°F as you can.

GARLIC BREAD

You'll be hard-pressed to find someone who doesn't like garlic bread.
This recipe makes a deliciously soft and fragrant loaf perfect for dinner parties and barbecues.

INGREDIENTS

350g Flour
250ml Water
7g Yeast
10g Sugar
5g Salt
15ml Vegetable Oil
Cilantro
Parsley
Dill / Chives
3 Cloves of Garlic
40ml Olive Oil

METHOD

Combine the water, yeast, flour, salt, sugar, and vegetable oil in a mixing bowl.
Knead the mixture until it forms a dough.
Chop the herbs. Peel and chop the cloves of garlic.
Place the herbs and garlic in a bowl, pour in the olive oil and salt. Mix well. Roll out the finished dough into an oval, spread the herb/garlic/oil/salt mixture over the surface, but don't use the entire mixture, leave a little bit to brush over the finished bread.
Roll the dough into a sausage-like shape. Cut the roll into 2 equal-length parts.
Plait the two parts of the dough together.
Grease the baking tray with oil. Put the dough onto the baking tray.
Preheat the oven to 350°F.

BAKING

Place the loaf in the oven.
Bake for 35-40 minutes. Transfer to a wire rack.
Coat the loaf with the remaining herb/garlic/oil mix.
Cool completely before serving.

Nutrition: Serving: 100g | Calories: 235.8 kcal

BAKER'S TIP

Serve warm with a pasta or chicken dish.

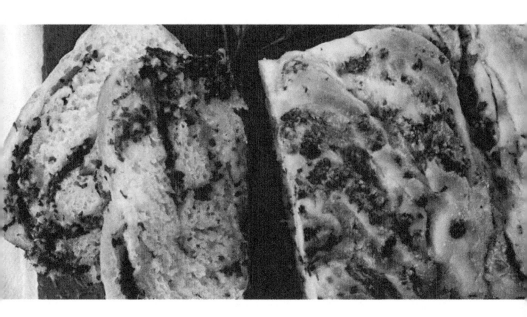

GLUTEN-FREE BREAD

A recipe for those people who love bread, but can't always eat it.

INGREDIENTS

250g Gluten-Free Bread Flour
125ml Cup Milk
180ml Warm Water
20g Butter (Softened)
15g Tbsp Sugar
5g Yeast

METHOD

Combine the dry ingredients.
Add the butter and mix through the flour. Add the warm water and milk.
Cover and leave to rest in a warm spot for 20 minutes.
Mix the dough again and then shape.
Prep your loaf tin. Line it with baking paper. Place dough into the loaf tin and allow it to proof for another hour.
Preheat the oven to 400°F.

BAKING

Cover with tin foil and bake for an hour.
Remove the foil and bake for another 10 minutes.
Transfer to a wire rack.
Cool completely before serving.

Nutrition: Serving: 1 slice (24g) | Calories: 70 kcal

BAKER'S TIP

Always let the bread cool before slicing.

CHAPTER THREE:

MORNING BREADS

BUTTERMILK BREAD

Buttermilk bread is the perfect addition to your breakfast menu. This recipe makes a deliciously soft and flavorful loaf.

INGREDIENTS

1kg Wheat Flour
3g Tsp Salt
15g Brown Sugar
10g Baking Powder
500ml Buttermilk (Room Temperature)
2 Eggs (Room Temperature)
125g Sunflower Seeds

METHOD

Preheat the oven to 350°F. Grease and flour a loaf tin.
Add all of the dry ingredients together. Mix the beaten egg into the buttermilk.
Combine the dry ingredients with the wet ingredients.
You should have a pourable dough. Add a bit of milk if necessary.
Pour the bread dough into the loaf tin.

BAKING

Bake for 50 minutes and then check to see how the bread is progressing. Place a wet cloth over the top and bake at 320°F for another 10-15 minutes.
Cool completely before removing from the tin.
This bread doesn't have a very long shelf-life, but can be frozen.

Nutrition: Serving: 1 slice (28g) | Calories: 80 kcal

ENGLISH MUFFINS

English muffins originated in the UK, but are eaten around the world. They are delicious toasted and smothered in butter.

INGREDIENTS

625g Flour 3g Instant Yeast 180ml Cups Milk
125ml Water 5g Butter 2g Salt

METHOD

Combine the flour, yeast, and salt.
In a separate bowl add the milk, water, and butter. Microwave for 20-30 seconds until the butter has melted, but don't let the mixture overheat.
Pour the wet ingredients into the dry ingredients and mix until you have a dough.
Don't worry if the dough is wet and sticks to your hands.
Now it's time to let your dough rise. Cover the bowl with cling wrap. It needs to stand for 12-18 hours at room temperature. After 12-18 hours, your dough will be twice the size it was.
Place it on a lightly floured counter. Leave to rest for a few minutes. Take a rolling pin and roll the dough out until it is about an inch in thickness.
Use a cookie cutter to cut the dough into round shapes. If you don't have a cookie cutter, use the top of a coffee mug or glass. Line a tray with baking paper.
Place the formed circles onto the paper as you go along.
Make sure that you place them far enough apart that they don't bake into each other. Once all the dough has been used, cover with cling wrap and leave for another 35-40 minutes.

BAKING

Use a non-stick pan on medium heat. Place the English muffins onto the pan and cover with a lid. Be gentle when moving so you don't knock out all the air.
You will most likely have to bake them in 2 to 3 batches, depending on the size of your pan. Bake for 5-7 minutes, then turn them over and bake for 4-5 minutes.

Cool completely before serving.

Nutrition: Serving: 1 muffin | Calories: 134 kcal

BAKER'S TIP

English muffins are great with both sweet and savory toppings.
Serve with butter and jam or scrambled eggs and bacon.

FINNISH OAT BREAD

A great twist on a health bread the whole family will enjoy.

INGREDIENTS

25g Tbsp Fresh Yeast
810g Cups Wheat Flour
5g Salt
320g Cup Oatmeal Flakes
500ml Warm Water

METHOD

First measure out the following ingredients:
- Flour 400g (+/- 20g)
- Oats 160g
- Water 500g

Pour the cereal into a bowl, add salt and yeast. Add the warm (40°) water.
Stir with a wooden spoon or spatula.
Leave to rest for 20 minutes. Cover the bowl with a lid so that the water does not cool down too quickly.
After 20 minutes, the oats should have swelled and the yeast will have bubbled.
Slowly add the flour little by little. The dough will be quite sticky, but don't worry.
There is no kneading to do for this recipe.
Prepare a loaf tin (use a silicone mold if you have one, as the bread expands quite a lot) and grease it well.
Transfer the dough into a mold. Use a wet spatula/spoon to help manage the sticky dough. Level the top.

BAKING

Place the loaf in a cold oven and set it to 440°F. Bake for 25-30 minutes.
Transfer to a wire rack.

Cool completely before serving.

Nutrition: Serving: 100g | Calories: 192.1 kcal

BAKER'S TIP

Add a delicious twist by sprinkling cinnamon sugar on top of the loaf before baking.

CLASSIC BAGELS

Bagels originated in the Jewish community in Poland. Now, they are a breakfast favorite throughout the world. Bagels are also the only bread that is boiled before it's baked.

INGREDIENTS

500ml Warm Water
2 pkts Active Dry Yeast
50g Brown Sugar
1.5kg All-Purpose Flour
10g Salt
10g Vegetable Oil
10g Yellow Cornmeal
Toasted Onions, Poppy Seeds, Sesame Seeds, Salt

METHOD

Add the yeast and sugar to the warm water. Stir until dissolved.
Slowly add 4 cups of the flour and the salt.
Add the rest of the flour in stages, 1/2 a cup at a time, and mix well after each addition. Turn out onto a lightly floured surface and knead until smooth and no longer sticky, about 5 minutes. Only add flour until the dough is no longer sticky.
Grease a large bowl and place the dough in the bowl. You can turn the dough in the bowl so that it is completely coated in oil. This will stop it sticking
to the sides of the bowl as it rises.
Cover with a cloth and leave in a warm place to rise for an hour.
Prepare a baking tray by greasing it with a teaspoon of oil.
After an hour, place the dough back on the floured surface. Punch it down and split into 12 equal pieces. Roll each piece into a ball and then each ball into a 6-inch log.
Join the ends, place fingers through the hole, and roll the ends together.
Repeat with all 12 pieces.
Place on the prepared baking sheet, cover, and let rest until risen, about 20 to 30 minutes.
Preheat oven to 400°F.

BAKING

Sprinkle cornflour onto a baking tray.
Bring 12 cups of water and the remaining tablespoon of sugar to a boil in a large pot.
In batches, add the bagels to the water and boil for 1 minute.
Dip the top of bagels in the toppings (poppy seeds, sesame seeds, onion, salt). Put the bagels onto the baking tray. Bake for 5 minutes, turn over, and bake for another 30 to 35 minutes.
Remove from the oven and let cool on a wire rack.
Cool completely before serving.

Nutrition: Serving: 1 bagel | Calories: 330 kcal

BAKER'S TIP

Remember that the wetter your dough is the more crisp your bagels will be, so make sure you don't add too much flour.

CHAPTER FOUR:
TEATIME LOAVES

GINGERBREAD

A classic teatime favorite and a popular bread to bake around the holidays.

INGREDIENTS

125g Soft Butter
125g Dark Brown Sugar
250ml Molasses
1 Medium-Large Egg 5ml Vanilla Extract
625g Cups Flour
8g Baking Soda
5g Ground Cinnamon
5g Ground Ginger
5g Ground Cloves
5g Salt
250ml Boiling Water

METHOD

Preheat the oven to 350°F.
Prepare your loaf tin by lining it with baking paper.
Combine butter and brown sugar in a large bowl. Use a mixer to combine them well and form a creamy mixture.
Add the molasses and stir well. Then, add the egg and the vanilla extract. Stir well.
In another bowl, whisk together flour, baking soda, ground cinnamon, ground ginger, ground cloves, and salt.
Mix the dry ingredients and the wet ingredients.
Carefully stir in boiling water until ingredients are combined and you have a nice, smooth mixture.

BAKING

Pour batter into the loaf tin and bake for 35-40 minutes.
Test by inserting a toothpick in the center. It should come out clean.
Cool before serving.

Nutrition: Serving: 1 slice | Calories: 400 kcal

Feel free to experiment with this recipe by adding different elements such as chocolate chips, cranberries, and nuts. You can also ice this loaf with a lemon drizzle.

PUMPKIN BREAD

A fragrant, spiced bread which makes a great teatime treat. Also the perfect addition to the Thanksgiving and holiday season.

INGREDIENTS

875g All-Purpose Flour
750g Sugar
250ml Vegetable Oil
4 Large Eggs
450g Pumpkin Puree
10g Salt
10g Baking Soda
5g Baking Powder
5g Ground Nutmeg
5g Ground Allspice
5g Ground Cinnamon
160ml Water

METHOD

Combine the sugar and oil in a bowl.
Whisk in the eggs and pumpkin until combined.
In another bowl, add the flour, baking soda, salt, baking powder, and all of the spices (cinnamon, nutmeg, allspice). Mix well.
Take half of the dry mixture and add it to the wet mixture. Stir well.
Add half of the water and stir. Then add the second half of the dry ingredients.
Separate the batter into two greased pans.
Preheat the oven to 350°F.

BAKING

Bake for about 1 hour or until the loaves are a nice golden brown.
Do a test to check that the cake is cooked through. Push toothpicks into the loaves.
If they come out clean, then the cake is baked.

If you notice the loaves are getting too brown but the cake isn't quite baked yet, shield the top with two pieces of tin foil.

Nutrition: Serving: 100g | Calories: 298 kcal

BAKER'S TIP

Spice it up by adding ingredients such as raisins, chocolate chips, or nuts.

BANANA BREAD

This recipe is a classic and a firm family favorite.

INGREDIENTS

100g Butter
250g Brown Sugar
2 Large Eggs
75ml Cup Milk
5ml Vanilla Extract
3 Ripe Bananas
500g All-Purpose Flour
5g Baking Soda
2g Teaspoon Salt

METHOD

Preheat the oven to 350°F. Grease and line with baking paper.
Melt the butter and combine it with the sugar. Add the eggs. Whisk
until they are completely combined. Add the milk and vanilla.
Mash in the bananas and add them to the mixture. You can mash
them quite smooth or leave them a bit chunkier, depending on what
you prefer.
Add the flour, baking soda, and salt. Combine all the ingredients
together.
Pour the batter into the lined loaf pans.

BAKING

Place the loaf pan in the oven.
Bake for 50 to 60 minutes.
After an hour, test with a toothpick/skewer to see if it's baked.
Cool completely before removing from the tin.

Place on a wire rack.
Store in a sealed, airtight container to retain moisture.

Nutrition: Serving: 1 slice (60g) | Calories: 196 kcal

BAKER'S TIP

Make sure to use bananas that are very ripe. This adds to the flavor.
You can also include 1/2 cup of chopped nuts or chocolate chips as
variation of this recipe.

CHAPTER FIVE:

FLATBREADS

SESAME BREAD

This recipe comes all the way from the shores of Zanzibar. A delicious, nutty flavored flatbread.

INGREDIENTS

900g Plain White Flour
1 Sachet of Yeast (about 7g)
500ml Coconut Milk
2 Eggs
2 Tbsp Sesame Seeds Salt

METHOD

Sieve the flour into a bowl. Combine all the ingredients with the exception of the sesame seeds. Knead the dough until it is smooth.
Place in a bowl and cover.
Leave the dough standing in a warm place for 30 minutes.
Roll the dough into balls in the palm of your hand.
Press them down flat.
Sprinkle with sesame seeds.

BAKING

Cook on a grill. Remember to turn them over so that both sides get toasted.

Nutrition: Serving: 1 slice (28g) | Calories: 30 kcal

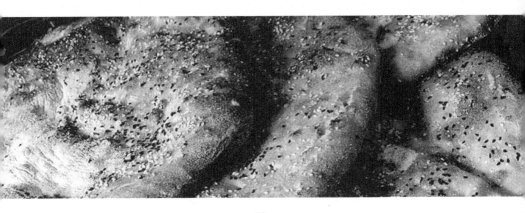

CHAPATIS

An unleavened flatbread, also known as Indian flatbread. It's the perfect accompaniment to curries and stews.

INGREDIENTS

230g Chapati Flour
3g Tsp Salt
5ml Olive Oil
Warm Water
Butter

METHOD

Combine the flour and the salt in a bowl.
Add the olive oil and enough warm water to make the dough workable, but not too wet.
Knead the dough with your hands until it is soft.
Place in a bowl and cover. Leave the dough standing in a warm place for 30 minutes.
Knead the dough a second time.
Roll the dough into balls in the palm of your hand and then press them down flat until they are about 3 inches thick.

COOKING

Use a frying pan with medium heat.
Cook the dough until it begins to puff up. Gently press it down with the spatula.
Turn over and repeat the process on the other side.
Once it is cooked, take it out of the pan and spread butter over it, then cover.

Nutrition: Serving: 1 | Calories:104 kcal

COOKING TIP

Chapatis can be easily stored and even frozen to enjoy later on.

CHEESE TORTILLAS

These can be easily adapted to include an array of delicious fillings, making them an adaptable recipe to add to your repertoire.

INGREDIENTS

125g Wheat Flour
125g Corn Flour
90ml Warm Water
15ml Olive Oil
10g Butter
12g Fresh Yeast
100g Cheddar Cheese (Grated)
15g Sugar
2g Salt
Dry Basil Leaves

METHOD

Combine flour, salt, sugar, and the yeast mixed in warm water.
Add olive oil to the dry mixture and knead the dough.
Place in a bowl, cover with cling wrap. Leave for 1 1/2 to 2 hours.
On a floured surface, roll the risen dough into a flat circle with an 8" diameter. Brush the surface of the dough with the olive oil and then add the grated cheese.
Sprinkle with dry basil.
Pinch the edges of the dough to the center, hiding the cheese inside.
Sprinkle a baking sheet with flour, put a tortilla on it, and place it in an oven preheated to 350°F.

BAKING

Bake for about 25 minutes or until golden brown.
Grease the finished tortilla with butter.
Cover with a cloth.

Nutrition: Serving: 1 (45g) | Calories: 140 kcal

BAKER'S TIP

Add scrambled eggs, bacon, and onion for a breakfast twist.

TURKISH FLATBREAD

Great with soups or as a snack with salads and cold meats for lunch.

INGREDIENTS

250g Flour
8g Baking Powder
200g Plain Yogurt
Any seeds or spices to taste, crushed or ground
(Cumin, Cilantro, Sesame, Mustard)

METHOD

Mix all ingredients to a smooth dough. It will be quite sticky, try not to add more flour.
Knead well (at least 5 minutes). Allow to rest for half an hour.
Divide into small balls. Roll out on a floured board as thinly as possible.

COOKING

Cook over high heat on a cast iron griddle or pan. Don't add oil or butter.
Turn over when it starts to puff-up.

Nutrition: Serving: 1 piece | Calories: 279 kcal

BAKER'S TIP

Fill with ground lamb, yogurt, feta cheese, bell peppers, and spinach.

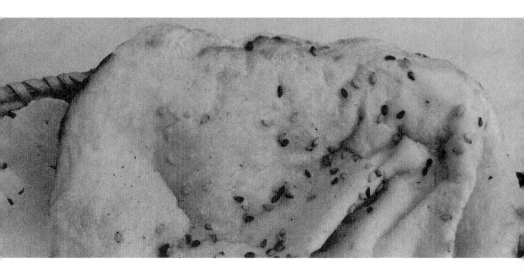

NAAN

Naan is mainly eaten in parts of Asia, Myanmar, and the Caribbean. It is a delicious addition to curries.

INGREDIENTS

250ml Warm Water
20g Honey
12g Dry Yeast
625g Cups All-Purpose Flour
75g Plain Yogurt
10g Salt
4g Baking Powder
1 Egg
40g Butter
3 Cloves Garlic, Finely Chopped

METHOD

Combine the warm water, yeast, and honey. Let it rest for a few minutes or until the yeast is foaming.
Using a mixer, add the flour, yogurt, salt, baking powder, and egg to the water, yeast, and honey mixture. Mix for a few minutes until the dough is completely combined and smooth.
Place the naan dough in a greased bowl, cover, and leave it in a warm area for 1 hour
(the dough will be about twice the size it was at the start).
While you are waiting for the dough to grow, you can cook the garlic in butter.
Infuse and strain.
After an hour, shape the dough into 6-8 small balls, then roll them out. They should be about a 1/4 inch in thickness.
Lightly brush the dough on both sides with the garlic-infused butter.

BAKING

Cook in a large pan. Make sure the pan isn't too hot. (Medium should be sufficient.) Add one piece of naan to the pan and cook for 1 minute or until golden.
Flip over and cook the other side.

Cover with a cloth to keep them moist.

Nutrition: Serving: 1 (160g) | Calories: 538 kcal

BAKER'S TIP

Add freshly chopped cilantro or parsley for a tasty twist.

GLOSSARY

Biga: a pre-fermentation process used in Italian baking.

Fermentation: when yeast reacts with sugar creating carbon dioxide and alcohol which helps dough to rise. The longer dough is given to ferment, the better the bread. Fermentation is also usually the first rest period.

Folding: a method of working the dough which helps the gluten to develop. The method involves laying the dough out and folding it in thirds, rotating it, and then folding again.

Gluten: a very important protein that holds the bread together. Gluten is found in wheat products such as flour.

Kneading: manually working the dough with your hands. Proof: the last rest period of the dough before baking.

Score: cutting the surface of the loaf prior to putting it in the oven. This gives the bread room to expand and not crack.

Sourdough: bread made with wild yeast.

Sponge: a type of pre-fermentation which mixes equal parts flour to water resulting in a wetter dough.

Starter: a combination of water and flour that promotes a healthy leaven. Starters work for many different breads.

EQUIPMENT CHECKLIST

While you may already have some of these items in your kitchen, you may want to add a few more to your Christmas wishlist.

- Digital Scale
- Oven & Kitchen Thermometer
- Starter
- Dough Scraper
- Large Mixing Bowl
- Measuring Cups
- Storage Container
- Proofing Basket
- Loaf Pan
- Silicone Mat
- Baking Stone or
- Steel
- Bread Knife
- Wire Cooling Rack
- Lame (blade to score bread)
- Stand Mixer
- Dutch Oven

REFERENCES

GLOSSARY OF BREAD BAKING TERMS

https://thelocalpalate.com/in-the-kitchen/glossary-of-bread-baking-terms/

RECIPES

https://www.povarenok.ru/recipes/show/129489/
https://www.povarenok.ru/recipes/show/50914/
https://www.povarenok.ru/recipes/show/79583/
https://www.povarenok.ru/recipes/show/64309/
https://www.povarenok.ru/recipes/show/64309/
https://sugarspunrun.com/gingerbread/
https://www.foodnetwork.com/recipes/pumpkin-bread-recipe-1957866
https://www.biggerbolderbaking.com/homemade-english-muffins/
https://tasty.co/recipe/homemade-dutch-oven-bread
https://www.foodnetwork.com/recipes/homemade-bagels-3644178
https://breadtopia.com/artisan-style-gluten-free-bread/

Printed in Great Britain
by Amazon